A Financial Guide To Help Widows

Noah H. Peterson

All rights reserved. Copyright © 2023 Noah H. Peterson

COPYRIGHT © 2023 Noah H. Peterson

All rights reserved.

No part of this book must be reproduced, stored in a retrieval system, or shared by any means, electronic, mechanical, photocopying, recording, or otherwise, without written permission from the publisher.

Every precaution has been taken in the preparation of this book; still the publisher and author assume no responsibility for errors or omissions. Nor do they assume any liability for damages resulting from the use of the information contained herein.

Legal Notice:

This book is copyright protected and is only meant for your individual use. You are not allowed to amend, distribute, sell, use, quote or paraphrase any of its part without the written consent of the author or publisher.

Introduction

This is a comprehensive and compassionate resource designed to assist women who have lost their husbands. The guide is organized into different sections, each addressing essential aspects of widowhood and providing practical guidance for navigating this difficult journey.

The Beginning section starts with an empowering quote, "A journey of a thousand miles begins with a single step," encouraging widows to take that first step forward. It covers important matters that need immediate attention, such as organ donation, notifications, and funeral arrangements. It also emphasizes the significance of family support and provides guidance on how to handle various aspects, including children and the husband's digital footprint.

Facing Your New Reality highlights the importance of taking charge and becoming informed about legal documents, including wills, trusts, and beneficiary designations. The guide offers advice on reviewing legal documents and understanding the role of trusts in estate planning.

Taking Inventory helps widows assess their financial situation, including assets and liabilities, as they prepare for the next steps in managing their husband's estate. This section provides an action list to guide the process.

Probate Court educates widows about the probate process, trust administration, and the settlement process for trusts. It emphasizes the importance of being cautious and thorough during this phase.

Building Your Team of Trusted Advisors advises widows on finding and hiring reputable legal, tax, and financial advisors to provide support during this challenging time.

Making Decisions guides widows in making financial decisions, creating a budget, and taking gradual steps to move forward.

Planning for offers guidance on planning for disability, updating estate plans, and choosing guardians and trustees for minor children. It highlights the importance of communication with family members about the plan.

The guide also includes a set of questions to ask when selecting an estate planning attorney, tax advisor, and financial advisor.

Throughout the guide, a Step-by-Step Journal encourages widows to record their thoughts and progress during each step of their journey. This journal serves as an emotional outlet and allows for self-reflection and growth.

The guide concludes with a section titled Moving Forward Toward New Journeys, emphasizing the importance of looking ahead and finding strength in embracing new opportunities and possibilities.

This book provides widows with the necessary tools and support to navigate the challenges of widowhood and embark on a path of healing and growth.

Contents

Step One The Beginning 1
  "A journey of a thousand milesbegins with a single step." 1
    So, let's begin. 2
    Organ Donation 3
    Notifications 3
    Funeral Arrangements 3
    Contact Family Advisors 4
    Family Matters 5
    Children 6
    Honoring Your Husband's Memory and Legacy 6
    Your Husband's Digital Footprint 7
Step One Action ListThe Beginning 9
Funeral Task List 10
Step-by-Step Journal 12
Step Two 13
You Are in Charge 13
  "She took a step and didn't want totake any more, but she did." 13
    Finding Your Legal Documents 14
    A Word of Caution About Legal Documents 15
    The Will 15
    Reviewing the Will 15
    Trust Agreements 16
    What is a Trust? 16
    Dry or Funded Trust? 17

Review the Trust	18
What if you can't find any estate planning documents?	19
If There Is No Will	19
Jointly-Owned Property	19
Beneficiary Designations	20
PODs and TODs	21
A Word about Organization	21
Step Two Action List Facing Your New Reality: You Are in Charge	22
Step-by-Step Journal	24
Step Three Taking Inventory	25
Step Three Action List Taking Inventory	28
LIABILITIES	31
MISC	31
Step-by-Step Journal	32
Step Four	33
Probate Court	33
Intestacy	34
Probate Steps	35
Trust Administration	37
Some Words of Caution	37
The Settlement Process for Trusts	37
The Seven Stages to a Trust Settlement	38
2. Valuation of Assets	38
3. Redemption of Insurance, Annuities, and Retirement Plans	38
4. Payment of Expenses and Claims	38
5. Tracking of Income	39
6. Payment of Taxes	39

    7. Distribution of Assets 39

    Taxes, Taxes, Taxes 39

Step Four Action List Pulling the Pieces Together 43

Step-by-Step Journal 44

Step Five Building Your Team of Trusted Advisors 45

    Legal Advisor 45

    How to Check a Lawyer's Record and License 46

    Some important questions to ask an attorney before hiring are listed in the Action List at the end of this chapter. 46

    Questions to ask a Tax Advisor before hiring are listed in the Action List at the end of this chapter. 47

    How to Check a Financial Advisor's Record and Licenses 47

    Questions to ask Financial Advisor before hiring are listed in the Action List at the end of this chapter. 48

Step Five Action List Building Your Team of Trusted Advisors 49

    Questions to ask an Estate Planning and Estate Administration Attorney before hiring: 49

    Questions to ask a Tax Advisor before hiring: 51

    Questions to ask a Financial Advisor before hiring: 51

Step-by-Step Journal 53

Step Six Making Decisions 54

  "Mostly it is loss which teaches us about the worth of things." 54

    Getting Started 55

    Create a Budget 56

    Stay Focused – Take Baby Steps 58

Step Six Action List Making Decisions 60

Step-by-Step Journal 62

Step Seven Planning for 63

- Planning for your disability 64
- Health Care Proxy, Directives, DNRs, and MOLSTs 64
- Power of Attorney 65
- Create an Estate Plan 66
- The Role of Wills and Trusts 66
- Selecting a Guardian and Trustee for Minor Children 67
- Tangible Personal Property Memorandum 67
- Update Beneficiary Designations 67
- Word of Caution – Minor Child Beneficiaries 67
- Discuss your Plan 68
- What's sharing too much? When to talk to your kids. 68
- Roles & Responsibilities 68
- Personal Representative 68
- Power of Attorney (POA) 69
- Health Care Proxy 69
- Guardian 69
- Trustee 69
- Disability Trustee 70
- Administrative Trustee 70

Step Seven Action ListPlanning for 71
- Questions to ask when selecting an Estate Planning Attorney 71
- QUESTIONS YOU MUST ANSWER AND PREPARATIONNEEDED FOR YOU TO EFFECTIVELY PURSUE ESTATEPLANNING 73

Step-by-Step Journal 75

Moving Forward Toward New Journeys 76

Step One
The Beginning

*"A journey of a thousand miles
begins with a single step."*
- Lao-Tzu

After losing your husband, it may feel more like "the end" than "the beginning" of anything. Nevertheless, you are at the beginning of a journey—the widow's journey. The path before you will be difficult and often painful. Not everyone will understand your grief and sorrow, nor will they know the best way to comfort you or encourage you to move forward. The initial shock of your loss may actually cause you to feel a temporary disconnect while you struggle to make sense of your new reality. The finality is jarring.

This is the first step on your widow's journey. During this first step, you are undoubtedly feeling overwhelmed and numb. And though this might feel like the worst time to have any responsibilities, there is work to do. In fact, there will be many family, financial, and legal matters that you will need to tend to throughout your entire first year as a new widow.

This book is designed to be your companion and guide as you navigate the confusion and decisions that will need to be made over the course of your first year as a widow. I have outlined Seven Steps that are intended to be batched as matters that should be addressed month by month. However, you may be ready to tackle the next step sooner or later than following a month-by-month approach. It's up to you to decide on the pace that is best for you, and it should be based on what you can handle.

The most important thing for you to understand is that these are the various matters that you will need to manage in the general order in which they will emerge and/or should be handled. Some matters might have time limits or time frames in which they should be taken care of. So, it will be helpful if you can work your way through the steps methodically, despite your emotional pain and where you are in the healing process.

This book will not make you an expert in the law, but it will help you understand the legalities required as you journey through post-death administration. The goal is to give you knowledge so you have more confidence to secure your investments and learn how to handle whatever money you have and build on it.

At the end of each chapter, I have included a few things to provide you with some extra support on your widow's journey. First, you will find a checklist of important actions that were presented in the chapter. Second, I have included some Helpful Resources (see page 125), that I hope will help to lighten your burden. And third, I have included some Step-by-Step Journal pages and writing prompts to help you to express your important feelings, emotions, and memories. My hope is that as you move forward, the Step-by-Step Journal will help you realize that you are making progress, so you gain strength and confidence.

So, let's begin.

What Needs to Be Done

If you have just lost your husband, there are many immediate decisions to make about the funeral. This is not easy, so you may want your friends and family to help you with these next steps.

Organ Donation

If your husband has just died, you are faced with the first most difficult set of decisions to make. Depending on the cause of death, you may need to decide about whether or not to donate your husband's organs. If you and your spouse have discussed this "what if" scenario, or if your spouse made a formal declaration, you may already know what your husband would have wanted. Even if he never mentioned his wishes, you can still make a decision that could give profound meaning to your loss and leave an enduring legacy.

Notifications

This is a painful task that you can delegate to a close family member. There are family, friends, employers (his and yours if your employer has a bereavement leave) and co-workers that must be notified in a timely fashion. If your husband was a member of a fraternal group, association, or club you may also wish to notify the group. You must also brace yourself for the onslaught of the same emotionally draining questions that you will be bombarded with repeatedly. Remember to ask for help with this from a friend or family member to preserve your energy.

Funeral Arrangements

The next big challenge is to make funeral arrangements. It can be particularly difficult to make these surreal choices at a time when it is hard to actually breathe. It may help to have a close family member or trusted best friend accompany you as you make funeral and memorial service arrangements.

You will come to understand the business side of funerals. There are also legalities about what can and cannot be done. The FTC also requires that a funeral provider must present customers with a General Price List (GPL) which is a statement that itemizes all of the services a person has chosen.

There are a range of decisions to be made involving the funeral as well as issues to manage before and after. At the end of this chapter there is a Funeral Task List to guide you through the overwhelming process of making key decisions.

Contact Family Advisors
There will be several financial, legal, and tax related decisions to be made over the course of your first year on this widow's journey. These decisions do not need to be made hastily or immediately. This is also not the right time for you to make any important life decisions. At this stage, it is just necessary to notify any professional advisors that your husband has passed. This is the beginning stage of determining what will need to be taken care of in short order, just not today.

If you do not have an attorney or tax advisor that is already handling your family affairs, you will need to start a search for the advisors that you will soon need. If you are ready to start discussing these important matters, and are ready to search for the advisors you will need, then please review Step Five on page 75. However, be sure to return to each section before Step Five, so you do not miss out on some important guidance that you may need as you begin to tackle the challenges ahead.

You will need several types of professional advisors, depending on what matters need to be addressed with your husband's estate. These include: an attorney (find one that specializes in estate planning, estate administration, and probate), an accountant (preferably a CPA – Certified Public Accountant), a financial advisor (preferably a Registered Investment Advisor with fiduciary responsibility) and maybe a corporate attorney if there is a business involved. I have included at the end of this chapter several resources to help you find qualified advisors.

Family Matters
A death in the family can bring out the best and sometimes the worst in people. You need to be prepared for both. You may have family members who might be reluctant to give you any "alone" time because they will worry about you. You may also have an array of interactions with your husband's family that could be either supportive or very hurtful. They too may be challenged by their own grief which can manifest itself in some ugly or unusual ways. You can acknowledge it, but you don't have to accept it. Don't hesitate to ask for help or space if that's what you need to get through the moment.

For example, take Terry. Her husband John died after a two-year battle with cancer. Terry and her husband had a young son together. When John passed, Terry's grief was excruciating for her because she was grieving for herself *and* for their young son. But Terry was shocked to find out that her in-laws shunned her because she reminded them of their loss, and instead wanted to have alone time with her son without her. It was devastating to her. Grief is powerful, and different people experience it very differently.

Family members and friends may also wish to receive some of his personal items for memory. Do your best to be true to your own needs and *delay* making any decisions involving the distribution of property to a future time. You may not yet want to let go of his things, and that is okay.

Be prepared for the world to start to get back to business, even though you feel like everything should stop. This may be a particularly sad and lonely time in contrast to when all of your family and friends were there to support you during the funeral. This could be the right time to consider meeting with a grief counselor or a support group. Even spending extra time with family and friends could help you through the very difficult days right after a funeral. I found that having a very full schedule was very helpful to me during the first few months.

Children
There are many things to consider if you have young children and extra help and guidance you will need. This is all outside the context of this book, but the Helpful Resources section at the back of this book lists several good books on the subject.

Honoring Your Husband's Memory and Legacy
Many widows find a sense of purpose, healing, and solace in taking action to create a memorial to their beloved spouse. These efforts can be as unique and diverse as you are and as your husband was. Here are just a few ways that you might consider to create an enduring legacy to your husband's life.

- Plant a tree in honor of your husband. This could be at a park or place of worship that had significance to your husband and family.
- Find an organization that is doing impactful work and find a way to create a gift to the group as a memorial to your husband.
- Create a family legacy album that captures the memories of your husband for future generations.
- Make a charitable donation in honor of your husband.

- You can have your husband's name inscribed on a memorial wall, garden bench, or gallery wall.
- Many local animal rescue shelters have legacy donor walls, or walk paths where a memorial donation could be made.

These are just some suggestions to get you thinking. However, your husband's life will provide the best ideas for what causes mattered most to him. By honoring his memory through his favorite causes, you can find a loving way for his memory to continue.

Your Husband's Digital Footprint
You may still be weeks away from tending to any important legal matters. However, there is one area that you should promptly address. If you have access to your husband's online passwords, it is a good idea close, freeze, or secure your husband's online accounts, including his social media accounts. (Facebook, LinkedIn, Twitter, etc.) You may decide to post his passing on Facebook and other sites since leaving the accounts active may become problematic and painful if they may result in business-related solicitations.

Keeping these accounts active can also create some vulnerability as you attempt to finalize your husband's estate and legal matters. Err on the side of caution and close these digital gaps. If you do not have access to your husband's passwords, you may need to seek the help of an attorney who has had experience in estate matters to help you manage the process necessary to protect your husband's legacy.

Your journey has just begun. As a trusted advisor to many, as well as being a widow, I know how difficult this first year will be and what needs to be done. I will do my best throughout this book to help you manage your journey and prepare for what challenges lie ahead.

Before you move forward to Step Two, please take some time to review the following sections:

- Step One Action List
- Funeral Task List
- Step-by-Step Journal
- Helpful Resources on page 125

Step One Action List
The Beginning

- ☐ Funeral notifications (delegate if possible).
    - Family
    - Friends
    - Employers, co-workers, business relations
    - Groups, clubs, affiliations, fraternal organizations

- ☐ Make funeral arrangements.
    - See the Funeral Task List on the next page.

- ☐ Contact your legal and tax advisors.
    - Contact Attorney
    - Contact Tax Advisor
    - If you do not have such advisors, then check the Helpful Resources on page 125 for links to find an advisor in your area.

- ☐ Manage family matters.
    - Can you delegate certain tasks in this chapter to family or trusted friends?
    - Children? Can a family member or a friend help you to manage some of your children's needs during this challenging time?

- ☐ Establish a memorial or legacy in your husband's honor.
    - Consider your husband's hobbies and memberships for inspiration.

- Talk to your friends about ideas.
- Ask your friends or family to research options for this.

☐ Secure all of your husband's digital assets and identity.

Funeral Task List

☐ Determine which funeral home will handle the arrangements.

☐ Schedule an appointment to meet with the Director.

☐ Determine if there are any special religious observances or protocols that you want included.

☐ Decide on where your spouse will be buried or interred.

☐ Decide what type of service you will have.

- This includes viewing, visitation, embalming, cremation or burial, purchase or rental of burial containers.

☐ Discuss the basic service fee and what it includes.

☐ Discuss and request an itemized list of all services and make payment arrangements.

☐ Ask someone to help you write an obituary.

- Review the obituary and ask others to review it.
- Publish it in the local paper and elsewhere as you deem appropriate.

☐ Provide the Funeral Services staff with information so they can publish the obituary notice.

☐ Make arrangements with their staff for any services they will help you with.

- Transportation
- Flower arrangements
- Clergy
  - What readings will be read
  - Who will do the readings
- Musicians

☐ Discuss with family who will be delivery eulogies, prayers, or helping as pallbearers or attendants.

☐ Make decisions about music to play or photographs to display.

☐ If there will be visitation or a wake, choose the clothes your husband will wear and delegate someone to deliver them to the funeral home.

☐ Delegate someone to update family on the date and time of the wake, memorial, and/or funeral.

☐ Delegate someone to secure refreshments for the visitation.

☐ Decide if you will have a post funeral luncheon or other type of gathering.

- Delegate the invitations to a friend or family member.

Step-by-Step Journal

Use this journal section to note your feelings, thoughts, and memories.

Here are some ideas that may be helpful starting points:
- ❖ If you were with me right now, this is what I would say to you…
- ❖ Today, I remembered the first time we met. My first impression of you was…
- ❖ What advice do you think your husband would give, to help you right now?

Step Two
Facing Your New Reality:
You Are in Charge

*"She took a step and didn't want to
take any more, but she did."*
- Markus Zusak,
The Book Thief

Right after your husband died, you probably woke up on some days thinking that this was all a bad dream—only to realize a few moments later that it was not a dream. This happens often to people who have suffered such an incredible loss. You might even feel as if your partner is just missing from you. I remember vivid dreams of finding Ron after a long search, only to wake up and realize it was just a dream.

It is probably really hard right now to imagine that you will have something to laugh about or will ever be really happy again. This is normal and just one of the many overpowering thoughts you will likely experience over the next several months. Despite what you may believe, to feel something, however painful, instead of numbness, means you are actually moving forward.

It is also very normal to feel angry. It could be anger that you lost someone who means so much to you or anger that you now have so many decisions to make and unexpected work to do while you grieve. This is all part of the baggage that comes with losing your spouse.

One thing that might help you now is connecting with others who understand your loss. I would strongly recommend that you spend at least one visit with a grief counselor if you haven't already done that yet. You might also consider a session with a grief group. Some widows discover that there is some comfort in spending time with others who are familiar with the pain you are experiencing. Just because you go once, doesn't mean you have to go back. You should decide for yourself if it helps or not.

What you must also begin to understand is that this is your new reality. I know that this might be very scary but remember to write down what you are actually afraid of. You have decisions to make because you are now in charge. You might not want to be in charge, but you are. You might long for the past when you and your husband may have made many decisions together, but you are at the beginning stage of a process that will allow your future to unfold. It is time for you to start pulling the pieces together so that you can protect yourself and be your own advocate.

Finding Your Legal Documents
Your first challenge is to find any family legal documents and to begin to organize your paperwork. Hopefully you and your husband maintained such documents in an easily accessible way, either in a secure place at home, a safe deposit box, or an attorney's office. If you aren't sure if there are any estate planning documents, or if you know they exist but do not know where they are, then this is the time to start looking for these important documents.

If you have a family attorney, check with their office since some attorneys retain clients' original estate planning documents.

Some of the documents to specifically look for include:

- ☐ A Last Will and Testament (the Will)
- ☐ Any Trust agreements
- ☐ Any other Estate Planning paperwork

A Word of Caution About Legal Documents
It is very important that you do not write on any legal documents that you find. You should also not remove any staples. These actions can create an opportunity for the validity of the documents to be contested. Also, you should consult with your legal advisor before destroying or disposing of any legal documents.

The Will
A Will is a legal document in which a person declares how their property (or assets) will be distributed when they die. It generally refers to property that is held in a person's individual name. If your husband did not have a Will, then his estate is considered "intestate" and his property will be distributed according to state probate laws. If he did create a Will then that should be submitted to the probate court so that his wishes and instructions can be recognized and then carried out. I will explain more about the probate process and what to expect in Step Four.

Reviewing the Will
If your husband did have a Will and you find it, you may wish to review it to get a sense of what he included in the Will. A Will is drafted in an arcane language that may be hard to understand, but you will be able to understand some parts of it. He should have identified who would be his chosen Personal Representative (the executor) to handle his estate and probate court requirements. There should be some reference to who will inherit his estate and whether there are any specific distributions to chosen beneficiaries. Take note of any assets mentioned so that you can include them when you look for account documentation in Step Three.

Many married couples prepare "I Love You" Wills. In "I Love You" Wills each spouse leaves their entire estate to the other. If the couple have children, their children are often the secondary beneficiaries. If you and your husband prepared "I Love You" Wills, you will likely be the sole beneficiary. You should also note that this means you will need to update your own current Will. I will expand more on what you will need to do to update your estate paperwork in Step Seven.

Eventually, you will be reviewing this document with your legal advisor to determine your rights and responsibilities. Once you move forward with your attorney, you will know what must be done and what will be required during the probate process.

Not all of your husband's assets will be considered probate assets and therefore will not "pass through" the Will or the probate process. As mentioned above, the Will and probate process involve assets that are held in a person's *individual* name and assets where the *estate* was listed as a designated beneficiary. Any assets that are owned *jointly* with others (such as a joint checking account) or assets that have a *designated* beneficiary (such as an IRA) are non-probate assets. I will explain the process in greater detail later in this chapter, and also in Step Four.

Trust Agreements
The next important type of document to look for is a trust agreement. Terms to look for are "Indenture of Trust" or "Revocable Trust" in identifying if you have a trust.

What is a Trust?
A trust is a document that is generally created during the life of the creator, also known as the trust maker, donor, grantor or settlor. The revocable trust is a common planning document created to provide a non-court process that governs who the manager (trustee) of the trust assets will be and who will be the beneficiary of the trust. Trusts also typically have provisions regarding disability and estate taxes.

Generally, a trust is a contract that the trust maker makes with the trustee to manage and distribute the trust assets. In a revocable trust, typically, the trust maker and the trustee are the same person during the life of the trust maker. The trust is a multi-chapter document that provides for instructions about who takes over as the trustee when the original trustee dies or becomes disabled, and who is the beneficiary of the trust in various situations.

Dry or Funded Trust?
Trusts can generally avoid court involvement at the death of the creator if the trust is *funded*. Do you know if you and your husband established any trust accounts at banks or financial institutions?

The revocable trust can be "dry" meaning that it does not own anything. The *dry* trust is a trust that the trust maker did not move assets into during his life. A *funded* trust is a trust where the trust maker transferred ownership and title to property into the name of the trust. For example, if you look at a bank account and it says something in this style: "John Quincy Adams Revocable Trust" then this indicates that the trust owns the account and therefore the trustee is in control of the account. If you review your deed or accounts and it just lists your joint names or your individual names, then it's likely that the trust is dry. Note that some states have a different process for funding trusts after the death of the trust maker so check with your attorney.

When a revocable trust is created, typically, the trust maker is the trustee. When the trust maker dies, the trustee must be replaced by a successor. The trust document should clearly indicate who the successor trustee is after the initial trustee is deceased.

If your husband did create one, you must first gather all of the trust paperwork and review the terms of the trust.

Important provisions in the trust are:

- ☐ Who is the named successor trustee?
- ☐ What do the terms say pertaining to distributions at death?
- ☐ Typically trusts outline what is to happen with the trust assets and when.

The next important issue when there is a trust is to make sure that you can identify the assets referred to in the trust and examine if they were *re-titled in the trust name*. In other words, you may need to determine if the trust was funded or whether it is dry.

One of the advantages of having a trust is that your affairs and the terms of the trust are *private*, unlike what happens during probate. The probate court process (which will be covered in Step Five) is generally a matter of *public* record. However, these are all legalities that you will discuss when you move forward with your attorney.

Review the Trust

Frequently, these documents are written in a language that is hard to understand. Don't worry about the details, just try to pull as much of this information together as you can.

- Do you have the original signed documents? If not, where are they? Frequently estate planning attorneys retain the originals for safe keeping, so check with the attorney.
- Determine if the trust is funded.
- Gather all account statements that verify what the trust owns:
  - Deeds
  - Account statements from:
    - Banks
    - Brokerage accounts
    - Investments

- What are the terms of the trust pertaining to *who* the successor trustee is?
- Who are the *beneficiaries*?
- Are there any parts that surprise you or cause you some concern?

What if you can't find any estate planning documents?
If you cannot find any documents, this is an additional problem because, in effect, you don't know what you don't know. Don't panic! Are you certain that you and your husband never prepared any estate planning documents? Or are you unsure if *he* ever did? Or do you think he did, but you do not know where the paperwork is? Depending on your answer, your attorney may be able to assist you with the process to find the answers to these important questions.

If There Is No Will
If you are able to determine that your husband indeed had no Will, his estate is considered "intestate." Intestate just means that a person died without a Will, and that your husband's assets or estate (anything that he owned *in his name only*) will be distributed according to your *state's* intestacy laws. Each state maintains its own intestacy laws, and I will cover this further in Step Four.

If your husband did not have a Will, there will be procedures to follow as his probate assets will be administered by the probate court process. However, there may be other assets that are not subject to the probate process. This includes jointly-owned property, life insurance, any retirement accounts, and any accounts that required a designation of a beneficiary. Look for any documentation of such assets to determine who is the named beneficiary or surviving owner.

Jointly-Owned Property

You and your husband likely have property that was jointly owned. It is common for couples to have assets that are held as JTWROS, which stands for Joint Tenants with Rights of Survivorship. This means that when one owner dies the property automatically transfers entirely to the surviving owner. This is generally property that you still have access to because you're named as one of the owners. Examples could include: a joint checking account, your home, and your car. You may also have financial accounts that are titled the same way. These assets may only require that you provide the custodian with a valid death certificate, so that they can change the ownership to you only and remove your husband's name.

Beneficiary Designations
There are also assets that do not pass through the probate process that are called "non-probate assets." These non-probate assets may have a specific beneficiary designation. Even if someone includes these assets in their Will with a different beneficiary instruction, *the only instructions that matter are the official ones maintained by the* **custodian of the assets**. Some examples include: life insurance, IRAs, 401(k)s, other retirement accounts, and savings accounts.

Generally, you will need to provide the custodian with a valid death certificate and then provide instructions for how you want to take possession of the assets. Especially with retirement accounts, there may be a variety of options with different tax implications, so *it is best to not make any decisions until you have consulted with your advisors*.

The important thing for you to understand, regardless of what you discover while searching for estate documents, is that you do not need to make any major decisions right now. This is your time to just pull the pieces together. Gather whatever you are able to find and start thinking about who you will need to help you as you move forward.

PODs and TODs

As you start to review your account statements from banks and investment companies, review the statements for words like POD which stands for "Payable-on-Death" or TOD which means "Transfer-on-Death." These designations may apply to specific assets or accounts so keep your eye open for these words on the statements you have for your accounts. At this point, just identify which assets or accounts have these POD or TOD designations, and highlight and flag them.

A Word about Organization

In Step Three, I will provide you with a more extensive list of potential family assets and financial paperwork for you to gather. You may have already started finding these items while looking for legal paperwork. As you find statements you should start to file them and label them, so you can easily refer back to them when you need to. One easy way to organize statements is by labelling a folder with the *custodian* or *issuer* of the statement. Then, within each folder you should organize statements chronologically.

If you're emotionally ready to start tackling the next steps in the legal process, then it is time to assemble your advisory team. You can review Step Five to find advice for gathering your advisory team. but please return to this step to make sure you have gathered all of the documents you will need to move forward.

Before you move forward to Step Three, please take some time to review the following pages:

- Step Two Action List
- Step-by-Step Journal
- Helpful Resources on page 125

Step Two Action List
Facing Your New Reality:
You Are in Charge

☐ Consider a single visit with a grief counselor or a grief group. Some places where you may get a referral from:

- Employer's Employee Assistance Program (EAP)
- Church or social center
- Local Hospital

☐ Start to look for any estate planning documents that your husband may have prepared such as:

- A Will
- A Trust
- Beneficiary designation forms for retirement accounts (IRA, 401K, annuities, and life insurance policies)
    - DO NOT WRITE ON any legal documents you find. Instead use sticky notes to flag items that you might have questions about.

☐ Start thinking about who might be able to help you as you navigate the next steps in the legal process.

- Make a list of your advisors:
    - Accountant/CPA
    - Lawyer
    - Financial Advisor
    - Insurance agent

- If you do not have any advisors that you are already working with, then review Step Five about how to choose your advisory team.

☐ Create a filing system to organize all of your statements, legal documents, and court-related paperwork.

- Get file folders, binders, and labels so you can easily organize and keep the paperwork in order.

☐ Organize any bank, investment, or life insurance statements that you find along the way.

- Organize by bank or institution
- File chronologically

☐ In many cases, the above information will be found on a computer:

- Properly-named folders
- Misnamed folders
- Scanned documents
- Emails
- Email attachments
- Sometimes as photo images
- Search on relevant keywords to find misplaced files.
- Get technical assistance if you need it.

Step-by-Step Journal

*Use this journal section to note your feelings,
thoughts, and memories.*

Here are some ideas that may be helpful starting points:
- ❖ I can't express how much I miss you. One thing I miss the most is…
- ❖ I am afraid of …
- ❖ One of my favorite memories of you is…

Step Three
Taking Inventory

"Everyone keeps telling me that time heals all wounds, but no one can tell me what I'm supposed to do right now. Right now, I can't sleep. It's right now that I can't eat. Right now, I still hear his voice and sense his presence even though I know he's not here. Right now, all I seem to do is cry. I know all about time and wounds healing, but even if I had all the time in the world, I still don't know what to do with all this hurt right now."
― Nina Guilbeau,
Too Many Sisters

Depending on what you discovered when you began searching for your husband's Will and any other estate planning paperwork, this process may have left you feeling a bit overwhelmed and stressed. Just the thought of having to think of your husband's life summed up by his "things" can be very painful. No matter what you found, Will or no Will, trust or no trust, there is still work to do. And even if there are no estate planning documents, there is still an established process and pathway to administering the estate.

Right now, the important thing to know is that you don't need to do this alone. By hiring the right attorney who *specializes* in estate planning, estate administration, and probate, you will have someone in your corner who knows what to expect and what to do next. Right now, your only challenge is to accept that this is your path. This is all part of the widow's journey. I too felt as if I just wanted to run away from everything. But know that *you have more strength and resilience than you realize.*

No one ever wants to hear that time heals all wounds. Just thinking that makes some widows feel as if they are allowing themselves to forget their lost loved one. But what you will discover (as all widows do) is that *you will always love* and *you will always remember*. And you will find that the injury from your loss will force you to become a stronger person than you were before. It is in that strength that you will find some version of peace that will enable you to move forward.

Now that you have started the process of gathering the important legal documents, your work continues. You will need to start finding and organizing all of the financial documentation of any assets and *liabilities* (debts) owned by you and your husband. This is the time to take inventory.

There isn't a lot of advice to give you at this stage. The most help you need right now is an easy checklist to know what types of documents to look for. For this chapter, your Step Three checklist will actually be your inventory checklist.

Do your best to gather any statements you find. Organize them by types of accounts, institutions, and in chronological order. Starting with tax returns is often helpful, since all tax forms should include an income statement (i.e. 1099s) for any accounts you and your husband had together. I recommend that you review several years of tax returns to make sure you have everything. If you and your husband had an accountant who prepared your returns, they may also have records and statements saved in their files.

Another good place to start is to check email and accounts for which you have passwords. Check your husband's computer and email for any account notices. If you find any accounts that have online statements, print out the recent statements and add them to your files.

As you review the bank and investment statements, be on the lookout for PODs (Payable-on-Death) or TODs (Transfer-on-Death) designations that I mentioned in the prior step. Typically, this language is listed on the paper statements received monthly, usually near the top of the page next to where the names appear. These designations mean that the account will pass directly to the person (or Trust) designated as the designee on the POD or TOD. These are very important designations to track. They should be noted and organized with the accounts that they apply to.

As you find any documents, be sure label them in files so you can quickly access the accounts. Keep in mind, that if the process becomes too overwhelming, you can ask a friend to help you or hire a professional organizer.

When you are ready to move forward with your attorney, these documents and statements will help your advisors to guide you as you establish your new financial foundation and your revised estate. Don't make any decisions regarding any of these accounts until you have evaluated all of your options and tax consequences with your advisor team. I will explain more about your team in greater detail in Step Five.

So, let's get started…

Step Three Action List
Taking Inventory

Financial Assets
Inventory Checklist

Use the following list as your guide to search for any assets or statements for each type of asset. Gather statements and any account documentation, including all account owner names and any beneficiary designation forms. Organize all documents, claim forms, along with account representative contact information, account numbers, etc., into file folders.

ASSETS
- ☐ Bank accounts
    - Checking accounts
    - Savings accounts
    - Money market accounts
    - Certificates of Deposit (due dates/terms)
    - Look for:
        - POD (Pay on Death) or TOD (Transfer on Death) Designations

- ☐ Safe deposit boxes

- ☐ Real estate and real estate ownership
    - Look for deeds

- ☐ Investment accounts
    - Stocks
    - Bonds
    - Mutual funds

- POD or TOD designations

☐ Stock certificates

- Some people still own the stock certificates for shares of stock.
    - Typically, they are large and colorful certificates. Pay attention to whose name is listed on the account.
- Some stock ownership transfers are managed by companies like Computershare or BNY Mellon, so look for statements from these companies (typically these are the main custodians for stocks not held in brokerage accounts).
- POD or TOD designations

☐ Retirements accounts

- IRAs (SEP, ROTH, SIMPLE)
- 401(k)s, 403(b)s, or other employer plans
- Pension accounts
- Any other employer benefits. Contact your husband's human resource department to determine what other benefits he was entitled to including pensions, life insurance, and accidental death insurance.
- Beneficiary Designations

☐ Annuities

- Qualified
- Non-qualified

- Any details about terms and withdrawal options
- Beneficiary Designations

☐ Life insurance

- Individual policies
- Employer group policies. Contact your husband's human resource department to determine what other benefits he was entitled to including pensions, life insurance and accidental death insurance.
- Key Man Insurance policies
- Any additional death or injury policies
- Beneficiary Designations

☐ Social Security records

☐ Veteran's Records & death benefits

☐ Military Records

☐ Digital Assets

- Email
- Social Media accounts (Facebook, LinkedIn, etc.)
- Personal websites
- Gather all passwords for all financial accounts.

☐ Business Interests

- Copyrights, patents, trademarks

- Company ownership – types of business structures:
  - Sole proprietorship
  - Partnerships
  - LLCs
  - S Corps
  - C Corps
- Buy-sell agreements (note all details)
- Crowdsource investments
- Websites or other accounts used for business ventures

☐ Title

- Cars
- Boats
- Other vehicles

LIABILITIES

☐ Mortgages (First, Second)

☐ Any Lines of Credit

☐ Credit cards (All)

☐ Student loans

☐ Any other debts

MISC

☐ Anything else you find, even if you aren't sure what it is.

Step-by-Step Journal

Use this journal section to note your feelings, thoughts, and memories.

Here are some ideas that may be helpful starting points:
- ❖ Some days I feel scared that…
- ❖ If you were still here, what I want you to know is…
- ❖ I am proud of myself because…

Step Four
Pulling the Pieces Together

*"No one can tell what goes on in between the person you were and the person you become. No one can chart that blue and lonely section of hell. There are no maps of the change.
You just come out the other side…."*
- Stephen King,
The Stand

By now, you may be feeling a bit anxious and overwhelmed by all of the documents that you needed to find and organize. You probably have so many questions about what you need to do and when. If you are ready to start working on your advisory team, you will find help in Step Five. But here I want to first give you some idea of what to expect as you move forward with the legal administration of your husband's estate.

As I have already shared, whether or not you were able to find legal documents and whether or not your husband created a Will or other legal instructions, there is a process to handle all of these affairs. Each state has *probate laws* that guide us on what must be done and when and who has the authority to handle such matters. There are specific procedures for when there is a Will, and for when there is not.

Probate Court
Probate and probate court confuse many people. Probate is a court process that is involved in proving the validity of a Will and carrying out its terms. The process exists so that once the Court can confirm that the Will is valid, it can appoint the *Personal Representative*, provide for the payment of the deceased's creditors, and assure that the Personal Representative is acting lawfully and making

distributions according to the terms of the Will. Probate is always the process that Wills have to go through in order for the Personal Representative to have the authority to act on behalf of the estate and distribute the estate assets to the appropriate parties. Probate is also the process used for the estate of anyone who died without a Will (intestate).

Intestacy

Sometimes when people discuss probate they also refer to intestacy or being intestate. This simply means that a person died without leaving a Will stating who should inherit their property. With or without a Will, a person's estate will pass through the probate court process, usually just called "probate."

If there is no Will, your husband's state of residence (or domicile) will have intestacy laws that will outline who can serve as the Personal Representative to manage the financial and legal affairs of the estate. The intestacy laws also outline who can inherit a person's property (and in what order) if there was no Will.

Generally, the estate of the deceased is *frozen* until the Personal Representative (also known as the executor) is appointed by the court. The typical beginning of the probate process is to *file a petition* with the court.

Once the Personal Representative is appointed, they will need to take inventory of all of the estate's assets. All the assets included in probate will require an appraisal. At the end of the process, debts of the estate and all creditor's claims on the estate must be settled with the available assets. After all the debts, taxes, and court costs are paid, the remaining assets are distributed according to the *intestacy schedule* based on the state's laws.

This entire process can be an overwhelming and confusing obligation. Although this process is usually straightforward, I highly recommend you hire an attorney. As a young widow and an attorney, I did not have the mental and emotional clarity to go through this process alone and hired an attorney to help me. Your legal advisor can guide you through the process and help you to understand the correct procedures and processes to complete these required steps, and save you countless headaches in the future.

If there is a Will, then the court will authorize the Personal Representative to distribute all property as outlined in the Will after all creditors, court costs, and taxes have been satisfied according to the process outlined below.

NOTE: Some states use the word Executor and some use Personal Representative, but they are interchangeable and represent the name of the person who has control over the deceased's estate assets. *Until appointed by the court, there is no one who has the authority to act on behalf of the estate.*

Probate Steps

There are certain things that you will need to do that your legal team will help guide you through. The basic probate process is outlined below:

- Filing a Petition to probate the will and appoint the Personal Representative.
- You will receive a "Letters of Authority" which is proof of your appointment from the court as Personal Representative. This is actually a single letter and will allow you to take care of the property and affairs of the estate.

- You (or your advisors) will need to secure a IRS identification number (EIN) for the estate.

- You will need to open an estate checking account to consolidate accounts and to pay creditors and disburse assets.

- You will need to keep accurate records of all transactions, payments, reimbursements, etc., including payments of expenses and any distributions made.

- You will need to prepare an inventory of all of the estate assets.

- For tax purposes, it is important that you know the value of the estate assets on the day of death (DOD).

- You will need to evaluate any creditor claims on the estate with your legal team. There are time limitations for how long creditors have to submit their claims. These claims can also be negotiated to reduce the claim.

- Your state may or may not require an estate tax return filing. Your legal and accounting team will guide you through any required federal filings or estate taxes.

- The estate will require a final accounting and closing statement.

- After all claims, taxes, and estate expenses are paid, the remaining estate assets can be disbursed to heirs according to the will.

The above list is daunting, even for someone who is not grieving. This is why it is important that you find an attorney who has experience with estate planning, estate administration, and probate to help you navigate this process.

Trust Administration

Even though trusts provide privacy for the family (versus the public nature of the probate process), there are still specific duties and responsibilities that the trustee must manage. And having a trust does not mean there will be no need to deal with the probate court. If any assets were not included in *and* funded into the trust, they will still be administered by the probate court.

Property does not transfer automatically just because there is a trust. There are still procedures to follow, documents to prepare, tax returns to file, and other matters that will need to be completed. Again, this is why it is important that your legal advisor is not a general practitioner but someone who specializes in estate matters.

Your attorney can help you to coordinate all aspects of a trust settlement including: payment of expenses, inventory and appraisal of assets, collection of insurance proceeds, and other matters specific to the trust.

Some Words of Caution

As you have been gathering documentation and having your initial conversations with some financial institutions, you may feel pressure to make some "easy" and "quick" decisions. One of the myths I encounter in this area of law is that some families believe that when a person dies, they should quickly close accounts, seal safe deposit boxes, etc. *It is very important that you don't close any accounts, change title on any assets, or make any decisions about retirement plans or IRAs until discussing matters with your legal advisor.* These are decisions that should only be made carefully, once you are aware of all of your options and any estate tax or other consequences of each option. The consequences can be huge.

The Settlement Process for Trusts

Similar to the probate estate administration process, there is a process to settling an estate when a trust agreement is in force. Generally, there are seven stages in the trust settlement process. How involved each step will be depends on the complexity of the estate.

The Seven Stages to a Trust Settlement

1. Inventory of Documents and Finances

This is basically what was described in Steps Two and Step Three of this book. You should have gathered both legal and financial documents and organized them for easy access and reference.

2. Valuation of Assets

For tax purposes, it is important that you know the value of the estate assets on the day of death (DOD). Federal estate tax rules provide the option to use an alternate valuation date. Your legal advisor can help you gather this information and determine which valuation date is the best option. States may vary on their rules for valuation dates.

3. Redemption of Insurance, Annuities, and Retirement Plans

For each custodian, gather any necessary claim forms. Be sure to have your legal and tax advisor guide you through any tax consequences for choosing any options available to you. Don't forget to check if any of your husband's credit cards included some life insurance or death benefit coverage.

4. Payment of Expenses and Claims

It is the trustee's responsibility to make sure that all expenses and claims are paid on behalf of the trust. You will need to stay organized and keep good records. You will need to maintain a ledger, and set up an estate checking account. Document any estate expenses that will need to be reimbursed by the trust.

5. Tracking of Income

In addition to tracking expenses, a trustee must also track any income (for examples: interest, dividends, loan repayments, final wages, etc.)

6. Payment of Taxes

This is an area where a trustee should rely on the guidance of a legal and tax advisor. There are a multiple tax matters that must be resolved accurately and filed properly.

7. Distribution of Assets

The final stage of the process is to distribute the assets of the estate. But this only happens after all debts have been paid, including:

- Estate and income taxes
- Advisor fees (legal, accounting, and other)
- Trustee fees and expenses
- All other administrative expenses

Your legal advisor can guide you through the proper order of these payments and distributions, as well as the record keeping and procedural requirements

Taxes, Taxes, Taxes

There are a number of taxes that will need to be addressed during the settlement of an estate. There will also be important deadlines and filings that you must be aware of. *This can be one of the most confusing and stressful elements of estate settlement. Keep in mind though, that you will not and should not attempt the tax issues on your own.* I strongly recommend that you consult a tax advisor that specializes in estate-related tax issues. Some of the taxes and tax-related issues to be aware of include:

- **Federal Estate Tax** – The estate tax is a transfer tax that is triggered when someone dies. There are exemptions including an Unlimited Marital Deduction that may be applicable. The deductions depend on who inherits estate assets and the amounts. The estate tax return (Form 706) is due nine months after death, but an automatic extension of six months is available.

- **State Estate Taxes** – Every state maintains different rules regarding state estate settlement and inheritance taxation. Your advisor can guide you through your state's requirements and filing deadlines.

- **Certain Assets** may not be included in the value of the estate and some assets may not be taxable. There can be many factors that must be considered and evaluated to determine if a tax obligation exists. For example, life insurance proceeds may be exempt from income tax but included in the estate valuation for estate tax calculation. Annuity distributions may be partially subject to income tax and included for estate tax purposes. Each asset in the estate must be evaluated for any tax obligation.

- **Retirement Assets** can also be complicated. Tax consequences will depend upon elections made by beneficiaries and the type of retirement account. It is best to not make any decisions or provide any election instructions until your advisor has outlined your options and the consequences of each.

- **Tax Basis** – During the settlement process you will encounter the issue of *tax basis*. An important tax classification is whether or not an asset receives a "step-up in basis." When a person inherits certain types of assets there is generally a readjustment of the value for tax purposes. Assets that have appreciated considerably during a person's lifetime, may be assigned a stepped-up cost basis when a beneficiary inherits the asset. If the asset receives a step-up in basis, the new higher valuation becomes the cost basis for the beneficiary. This saves the estate capital gains tax on the asset appreciation. Not all assets are eligible for a stepped-up basis so this is an important conversation to have with your advisors.

- **Final Income Tax Returns** will need to be filed. Be sure to gather tax returns for the trust maker's last three years.

- **Significant Gifts** – If any were made during the year, a gift tax return may also need to be filed.

- **Real Estate Taxes and Personal Property Taxes** may also need to be paid.

In addition to these various obligations and issues that must be tended to during the settlement of an estate, *there may also be a variety of filings and requirements for your individual state.* The important thing is to know that your trusted advisors can guide you through this process to minimize the stress and to help you make the decisions that are in your best interest. The next step will address how to find and hire your advisors.

Step Four Action List
Pulling the Pieces Together

☐ If you have yet not gathered and organized the documents noted in Step Two and Step Three, now is the time to make sure you have all of the documents and statements you have access to.

☐ Take the time to carefully organize all of the documentation in labeled files to make everything easy to find when you need it.

☐ Track expenses related to the estate carefully.

☐ Ask the bank for a Date of Death value for any accounts held by the bank.

☐ Contact your accountant regarding filing deadlines

- Note in your calendar the dues dates for tax filings

Step-by-Step Journal

Use this journal section to note your feelings, thoughts, and memories.

Here are some ideas that may be helpful starting points:
- ❖ I never told you that…
- ❖ If I had died, leaving you to pick up the pieces, I would give you this advice:
- ❖ It felt strange, but today, I smiled when…

Step Five
Building Your Team of Trusted Advisors

"When walking alone in a jungle of true darkness, there are three things that can show you the way: instinct to survive, the knowledge of navigation, creative imagination. Without them, you are lost."
― Toba Beta,
My Ancestor Was an Ancient Astronaut

Now that you have done the important job of gathering all of the legal documentation and statements that you have access to, it is time to select your team of advisors to help you begin to take care of settling your husband's estate. You and your husband may already have some of advisors that you will need. The important thing is to make sure that you are working with professionals who have experience in estate planning and estate administration issues.

Legal Advisor
Your legal advisor should be an attorney who specializes in estate planning, estate administration, and probate. Even if a general practice family attorney prepared any estate documents for you and your husband in the past, it would be best to have an expert in these matters going forward. A medical analogy would be that you would let your primary care physician prescribe blood pressure medicine for you, but if you needed heart surgery, you would look for a cardiac surgeon.

Your legal advisor can guide you through the bulk of issues that come with estate settlement. They can help you manage your records, help with creditors, oversee the tax filings, and help you to manage all of your legal obligations.

How to Check a Lawyer's Record and License

Before hiring an attorney, it is always a good idea to verify that they are licensed to practice in your state. You should also verify if they have insurance. By checking an attorney's license, background, credentials, reputation, and complaint and disciplinary action record, you can protect yourself from potential problems. You should contact your state's attorney registration department or state bar association to check the attorney's record.

The Helpful Resources section on page 125 includes a database source to help you find your state's agency, bar, or disciplinary committee. For example, I practice in Massachusetts, where the Attorney Status Reports are maintained by the Board of Bar Overseers. (http://massbbo.org) These *bar organization reports* indicate if an attorney is actively licensed to practice in the state, if they are covered by professional liability insurance, and if there is any record of disciplinary action.

Some important questions to ask an attorney before hiring are listed in the Action List at the end of this chapter.

Tax Advisor

If you already have a family accountant who has been handling your tax filings, they may be the best choice to help you as tax matters need to be addressed. However, you may also want to find out if your accountant's firm has someone in their office that specializes in handling estate-related tax matters. If you don't have a tax advisor, you should include one in your professional search. Your tax advisor can work with your attorney to manage the tax filings and decisions. I would recommend using an accountant that has earned a CPA (Certified Public Accountant) designation. The Helpful Resources section on page 125 includes sources to verify the licensing and disciplinary record for CPAs.

Questions to ask a Tax Advisor before hiring are listed in the Action List at the end of this chapter.

Financial Advisor

It would be wise to include a financial advisor on your team to help you manage the financial and investment decisions that will need to be made as you move forward with your own adjusted estate. The important caveat is to be extra diligent in your selection by choosing an advisor that has a *fiduciary responsibility* to advise in your best interest. There are numerous types of professionals in the financial services industry. Some are simply licensed sales people who only have a duty of "suitability." As long as an investment is considered suitable, whether it is in your best interest or not, they can recommend it. An advisor with an RIA (Registered Investment Advisor) designation is bound by *fiduciary* rules. This means, just like an attorney, they are held to the highest standard of care for you.

Your financial advisor can help you to evaluate your options as you take control of the assets that you have inherited. They can guide you through the best strategies to manage the changes to your family income and budget.

This can be a very scary time for many widows since their entire financial outlook has changed. You may need to make adjustments to assure that you have the resources and income you need to maintain your home and expenses. This may also require that you make some short-term decisions and then work toward long-term solutions that will serve you best moving forward.

How to Check a Financial Advisor's Record and Licenses

Before hiring a Financial Advisor, it is always a good idea to verify and check their record just as you would for an attorney. The Financial Industry Regulatory Authority (FINRA) maintains a Broker

Check database so you can verify an advisor's employment history, license status, and record of any complaints and disciplinary actions. The Securities and Exchange Commission (SEC) also maintains a database on Registered Investment Advisors. Links to the FINRA and SEC background check sites are listed in the Helpful Resources section on page 125.

Questions to ask Financial Advisor before hiring are listed in the Action List at the end of this chapter.

Team Approach

It is in your best interest to assemble a team that can work *together* on your behalf. Not only will you need legal advice, you may also require tax advice and financial/investment advice. There will be decisions that require the coordinated guidance of two or more types of experts, so it is always best if you have advisors that work well together *on your behalf*. You may also find an advisor that is an expert in more than one required expertise, which can reduce miscommunications within your group of advisors and speed things up. On page 125, I have included some Helpful Resources to help you find qualified advisors in your area.

Finding the right advisors to help you is your only task for this step. The first advisors you encounter may not be the best qualified to guide you through this challenging time. Save yourself any additional hardship or regrets by taking the time to assure that the professionals you choose to work with are qualified to help you.

Step Five Action List
Building Your Team of Trusted Advisors

☐ Check the advisor search resources on page 125.

☐ Create a short list of candidates for:

- Legal
- Tax/Accounting
- Financial/Investments

☐ Contact the candidates and interview them for consideration to be part of your team.

☐ Refer to the questions listed below when you interview each professional under consideration.

☐ Verify each professional's license, background, complaint or disciplinary record, etc.

☐ Make your selections and set up appointments to get started.

Questions to ask an Estate Planning and Estate Administration Attorney before hiring:

☐ How long have you been in practice?

☐ Do you specialize in in estate planning and estate administration?

☐ What is your experience in **Probate and Trust Administration**?

☐ Please tell me about your interest, background, and experience in the **Probate and Trust Administration** field. What percentage of your practice is in **Probate and Trust Administration**?

☐ Can you help me coordinate the **Probate or Trust Administration** with the other advisors on my team, such as an investment and tax advisor?

☐ How do you bill for these services?

☐ Are you fee-based or hourly?

☐ What is the time frame and process for administering this estate or trust?

☐ What does it cost?

☐ How will you communicate with me during this process?

☐ Who will be my main contact during this process?

☐ How often do you review plans with clients and communicate status updates?

☐ What are the expenses to maintain and update my legal documents?

☐ Do you have malpractice insurance?

☐ What happens if something happens to you the attorney?

☐ Do you handle the filing of estate tax returns if they are necessary?

- If you do, how do you charge for that service?

- [ ] How do I prepare for our consultation?

Questions to ask a Tax Advisor before hiring:

- [ ] How long have you been in practice?
- [ ] Do you have a specialty or type of client you work with most?
- [ ] Do you have any special training or experience handling taxes for financial and estate plans and estate administration?
- [ ] Are you certified (CPA)?
- [ ] How do you charge for services (fee-for-service or hourly)?
- [ ] Do you provide *year-round* consulting, monitoring, updates, and account servicing?

Questions to ask a Financial Advisor before hiring:

- [ ] How long have you been in practice?
- [ ] What financial training have you received?
- [ ] What licenses and registrations do you have?
- [ ] What sources of information do you use to make recommendations?
- [ ] How are you compensated for your services?
  - Do you charge commissions on the front end (when investments are made) or back end (when investments are sold)?

- Do you earn compensation from offering me certain investment products?
- Do you charge a fee for your services, and if so, what is it and how is it calculated?
- Are there any additional account or management fees for working with you?

☐ How often do you review plans with clients and communicate status updates?

Step-by-Step Journal

Use this journal section to note your feelings, thoughts, and memories.

Here are some ideas that may be helpful starting points:
- Before we got married, I used to always_____and I think I want to try that again.
- Today I am thankful that…

Step Six
Making Decisions

*"Mostly it is loss which teaches us
about the worth of things."*
— Arthur Schopenhauer,
Parerga and Paralipomena

You may not realize it, but if you have done the various tasks and journaling outlined so far in this book, you should be very proud of yourself. This is a lot to handle under the best of conditions. And you have managed to take the necessary steps to do what needs to be done, despite the enormous challenge.

This next step is for you and about you. It involves understanding what you have, the income available to you, and how to take care of your loved ones in your new life.

In my experience, it is the fear of the unknown that keeps us stuck. Healing and growth begin when you get your mind in gear and start to move forward with clarity. This next step is usually a huge stress point because it involves confronting the future and your relationship with money.

Many women have not had the role of being the financial "partner," so this step of creating a budget may seem like a daunting task, since it will require that you develop a relationship with your money that you may not have had before. And figuring out what you can afford in your new situation can be stressful. Some women may appreciate the freedom to define how their money is allocated, but for many this process may need to begin with a basic understanding of their income, identifying expenses, and then slowly tying the two together.

I recall a client Mary whose husband died after a battle with cancer. Although she had time to prepare for the loss, it was only after her husband died that the truth was revealed. Her husband had massive debt. Fortunately, it was not her debt, and her home was secure. Nevertheless, it was crushing to not only discover that there were very few assets in the estate, but also to confront the truth behind the debt that her husband had hidden from her.

Thankfully, she was able to overcome the loss of her husband and to take financial control by setting out to create a new career path for herself in her early sixties. At first her new career was driven by the need to generate more income, but ultimately it gave her a new and fulfilling life, with new friends and new adventures.

Losing a spouse shatters the vision of the life you had planned, as well as sapping the energy you received from sharing your life with someone else. Before, you had someone to change the oil in the car, shovel the walk, fix the leaking faucet, or deal with the heat if it's not working. Yes, your new life situation will be stressful with new responsibilities, but take a moment to reframe it. *This is an opportunity to re-invent yourself*.

So now it's time to get started in creating a household budget that will allow you to create a new vision of the life you want to have.

Getting Started
I hope by now you have all of your legal documents and financial statements in order and organized for easy retrieval. You should also have tax statements and contact information for each of the financial accounts and the professionals who will be guiding you through the next steps. *I also recommend that you maintain a single notebook to take notes at all of your meetings with your advisors.* Use this to keep track of any questions you have, answers you

receive, and make a record of what others will be doing and what you should be doing.

This will help you to stay organized, especially when there is still so much emotional challenge in dealing with all of these matters. If you have a solid financial plan, you can focus more of your energy on working through your grief rather than worrying about how to make ends meet.

Create a Budget

As you begin meeting with your advisors, some of the first issues to address are what resources you actually have access to for household maintenance and your everyday expenses. Your advisors can walk you through what your options are for managing these short-term needs and what you need to do for your ongoing and long-term needs. *It is very common that the loss of a spouse also means that there is a loss of income, whether it is from employment or social security.*

Your own income planning needs to be one of the first matters that you address. You and your advisors have already started to assess your husband's estate and any life insurance proceeds and joint assets that you already have access to, so you should have some basic information available already. It helps if you prepare a budget to take to your meeting with advisors, so start by preparing a record of your current sources of income and all of your fixed, variable, and seasonal expenses. This will help you to determine what may need to be done to assure that you have adequate income to meet your living expenses. This basic budget information will help shape the best investment options for your needs.

It is likely that you will receive the bulk of your husband's estate. It is quite possible that the investment objectives that you had as a couple may not be the same objectives that will serve your needs as a widow. You will need to discuss your own financial goals and objectives with your advisors to begin to shape a plan that will serve *your* financial plan and goals.

Timing and taxes will be big issues to consider. There will be a projected schedule for when you will have access to different estate assets. There will be tax issues and planning for you to consider as you decide if there should be any changes in the investment mix of your holdings.

Your own retirement planning should also be reassessed. You may have options to take rollovers, lump-sum distributions, or lifetime annuity payouts from inherited retirement assets. You should review all of your options carefully with your team so that you understand the short-term and long-term tax implications of the various options available to you.

This will be a time of taking action and making decisions. You and your team will start taking care of the various estate administration matters.

There are a few parties you will have to contact:

- You will be contacting the custodians of the estate accounts, social security, and your husband's retirement account managers.

- You will be giving notice, providing death certificates, giving instructions, and taking care of putting the pieces back together as you create the foundation for your own estate.

- There will be probate matters, creditor payments, and tax filings.

This is all part of the process. There will be many financial planning decisions that you will have to make. Having someone to talk to and guide you will be enormously helpful. Your attorney will help guide you through the legal decisions that you will need to make as they need to be addressed. Your attorney will also advise you on matters that need to be directed to your tax advisor and investment advisor regarding your individual situation. Hopefully, you now know what to expect and you are more emotionally ready to start the work that comes with this part of the widow's journey.

Stay Focused – Take Baby Steps
In my life and in my practice, I have learned that large projects and big decisions are really difficult, but what has worked very effectively is breaking a project into small steps—baby steps—to tackle each day as part of a *daily ritual*. What's amazing is that it is so much easier to get things done when the tasks are broken down to small, clearly-defined tasks. Write each task on your list as if you were instructing someone else to do it. Before you know it, the large project is done, and the feeling of accomplishment is enormous!

So, consider further breaking down each of the steps outlined, into even smaller steps. For example, the process of creating a budget is a big project. Perhaps start by just deciding that you will sit down daily for 10 minutes at the *same time* in the *same place*. Then begin with finding the utility bills for your electricity for the last 12 months. The next day, look for the cable bill. The next will be water/sewer and so on. By the end of the week you will be on your way to having a better sense of where your money is being spent.

You must know what you have in income and what you spend otherwise you will be in fear of how little money you have, even if it's sufficient for your needs. In this stage, you have to face the facts of this new reality. The longer you hide from this, the longer it will take you to move forward. You will learn that you are capable of many things, and this process will help you redefine who you are. Everything will not be perfect, but nothing ever is perfect! Change is not always bad, but it is hard for most of us, since it involves the fear of the unknown.

One of my dearest clients lost her husband in 2009 after a bold battle with brain cancer. In the years that followed, Evelyn slowly adjusted to her new life. When I spoke with her about this book, she told me that at seventy-three she had finally found a little dream home that was all her own. Despite living in many grand and extravagant homes with her first husband, now for the first time, at seventy-three, she was able to create the home that she had wanted and had envisioned all of her life. The change was not instant, but rather, required an evolution of her thinking and an acceptance of her new life and of the control it gave her. This allowed her to have the life she had always dreamed of.

Sometimes it is hard to stop in the moment to realize that we have changed or that we have grown. It is in this time and space that you will be starting to heal. This experience has impacted and redefined your life and will continue to do so. What you have endured is one of the most difficult experiences in life. *So, take time to be proud of yourself for your strength and resilience.*

The following Step Six Action List itemizes the various items that you need to pull together to help you create a budget.

Step Six Action List
Making Decisions

☐ Prepare a new household budget. Itemize the following:

- All of your sources of income. Look at your tax returns for three years.
    - Salary
    - Social Security
    - Pension benefits
    - IRAs
    - Investment dividends and interest
    - VA benefits
    - Rental income
    - Royalty income
    - Other income.

- All of your fixed, seasonal, annual, and discretionary expenses.
    - Housing
        - Rent
        - Mortgage payment
        - Homeowners/Renters Insurance
        - Expenses you pay to maintain your home (Condo fees, Parking Fees)
        - Real estate taxes
    - Utility expenses
        - Electricity
        - Oil/Gas Heat
        - Water/Sewer
        - Internet

- Cable
- Phone
    - Food Expenses
        - Groceries
        - Restaurant
    - Transportation
        - Car payments
        - Car insurance
    - Debt repayment
        - Credit cards
        - Car loan
        - Education loans
    - Health Insurance
        - Co-Pays
        - Prescription medications
    - Clothing
    - Entertainment
    - Income taxes

☐   Organize the income and expense information to share with your financial advisor.

☐   Think about your own financial objectives and retirement objectives.

☐   Start a notebook to keep records of your meetings, action items, and questions.

☐   Start to work with your team to address all of the steps to completing probate and administering your husband's estate.

Step-by-Step Journal

Use this journal section to note your feelings, thoughts, and memories.

Here are some ideas that may be helpful starting points:
- ❖ During this widow's journey, I have discovered that I…
- ❖ I never thought I would be able to…
- ❖ The hardest thing I have ever had to do was…

Step Seven
Planning for
Your Loved Ones

"Every widow wakes one morning,
perhaps after years of pure and unwavering grieving,
to realize she slept a good night's sleep,
and will be able to eat breakfast,
and doesn't hear her husband's ghost all the time,
but only some of the time.
Her grief is replaced with a useful sadness…
we learn to live in that love."
— Jonathan Safran Foer,
Everything Is Illuminated

Losing a husband is really one of life's most difficult wounds. You have been jettisoned upon a widow's journey—one of the most heartbreaking and emotionally devastating experiences you can endure. But by allowing yourself to learn the best way to manage the obligatory legal, financial, and tax burdens of your husband's estate, you have shown grace and wisdom in taking care of what needs to be done.

Now it is time to take that wisdom and all that you have learned during this process to decide what you should now do for your loved ones. Whether your husband made sure that everything was in order so you had less to worry about, or if he didn't do any planning at all and left you with a lot to learn and to do—this will shape how you approach your own estate and what you can do for your own heirs.

No doubt, this has been a learning experience. Many clients who have come to me through such a loss want to make sure that their family members are protected and will not have to go through a similar process (especially if it was an estate without a plan). It's now time to create a plan for your family that will protect them and prevent much of the pain and stress you just went through.

If things went well, you have chosen a legal, tax, and financial team that you trust and have confidence in. You have come to know and understand them during this process and they can now begin to help you to *clarify your own legacy and your own plans to care for your loved ones.*

Planning for your disability

You will need to do planning that will shape your remaining years and your legacy. The first aspect of planning is determining who will be the person you entrust with making lifetime decisions for you if you become incapacitated. If for any reason, you were to become incapacitated or unable to handle your own financial affairs or medical decisions, who would you want to take care of you and your affairs?

Health Care Proxy, Directives, DNRs, and MOLSTs

An Advance Health Care Directive (also known as a Health Care Proxy) is a legal document in which you declare who you would want to make decisions about your medical care if you are unable to do so.

Many health care providers will ask you if you have any health directives and proper documentation. They will then have this information on file, if needed. If you are hospitalized or are in a situation where your medical providers determine that you are unable to advocate on your own behalf, then they will contact your chosen proxy for guidance and health care decisions. *Authority does not transfer to your proxy unless and until you lose capacity* to make health care decisions.

If your health deteriorates to the point that end of life decisions need to be made, the medical providers will follow the mandates of your written instructions. One such document is referred to as a DNR legal order, which stands for "Do Not Resuscitate." This means that the medical team must allow for a natural death. They are prevented from performing CPR (cardiopulmonary resuscitation) or ACLS (advanced cardiac life support) if your breathing or heart stops.

In some states (NY, MA, CT, RI, MD, and OH) a MOLST (Medical Orders for Life-Sustaining Treatment) Form is also available to provide active medical orders. These documents are signed *while you have capacity* and are effective immediately.

Aside from executing these document, I highly recommend that you let your chosen proxy know that you have given them this authority, and you directly explain your health care and end of life wishes. End of life wishes are typically embodied in a document called a Living Will. Talk to them from the heart, and tell them what you would really want to have happen in these medical situations. This will give them the peace of mind and certainty needed to make the right decision for you, based on what you really wanted for yourself.

Power of Attorney
A "power of attorney" (POA) is a legal document in which you choose someone to handle your financial and business affairs if you are unable to handle them yourself due to incapacity (or at any other time that you determine that authority should start). Your POA should make it very clear when the authority begins and what your agent has the authority to manage on your behalf. It is important that you have a durable power of attorney, since "durable" means that the POA will survive during your incapacity—which is a time when

you will need it to be already in place. These rules are state specific, so discuss this with your attorney.

Create an Estate Plan
This entire experience you are enduring demonstrates how important it is for everyone to have an estate plan. Regardless of the size of an estate, there are important decisions that need to be made in advance to assure that your desired wishes are documented and honored.

The Role of Wills and Trusts
A Will is a formal document that designates who you want to be in control of your estate when you die, and who you want to receive your estate. If you have minor children, the Will is the document you need to designate who you want to act as their guardian. The courts are involved to monitor the administration of estates. A trust may also play an important role in an estate plan. Trusts are helpful in maintaining privacy and providing careful instructions for how and when beneficiaries will receive their inheritance. Assets held in trust are *not* part of the public probate court proceedings.

As you evaluate your current estate with your advisors, you may determine that your instructions must be documented or updated. For example, if you do not have a Will, then you should create one. If you do have a Will, whenever there is a major life change, such as losing a spouse (or any asset changes), then your Will should be updated to reflect your current situation, assets, and wishes.

If a trust is needed to build your estate plan, you now understand how important it is for your assets to be properly "retitled" to the trust so that the trust is *funded*. In many situations involving children, a trust facilitates passing an inheritance to the children (minors and adults) while protecting them from predators, creditors, and perhaps themselves.

Selecting a Guardian and Trustee for Minor Children

As noted above, a guardian is the person with whom your minor children will live if you die. The guardian does not typically have any control over the child's estate (what they inherit from you). I usually recommend that a client who has minor children set up a trust and name a trustee to oversee the child's estate. A trust allows to you determine how your money is to be used for your child and when the child will ultimately inherit the estate. A trust can be built into a Will (a "testamentary trust") or be created as a separate document during life (an "inter vivos" or "living trust").

Tangible Personal Property Memorandum

Talk to your attorney about how to document who gets your personal tangible property. Tangible property is anything you can literally touch, like jewelry or furniture. We recommend that you make a list of who gets what in a document called a Tangible Personal Property Memorandum and put it with your estate planning documents.

Update Beneficiary Designations

If you have life insurance, retirement accounts, or any other accounts with Designated Beneficiaries, the designations must be reviewed and updated if necessary.

Word of Caution – Minor Child Beneficiaries

You should not name minor children as direct beneficiaries of life insurance policies. Generally, *a life insurance company will not pay out life insurance benefits to a minor child*. The life insurance company will require that a conservator be named and the life insurance proceeds will only be paid out when the conservator is appointed. A conservator is someone who is appointed through the court process to manage the child's estate until they are 18 years old. In Massachusetts, this is *a long and expensive process*. In some states, the process might be easier, so please consult with your local attorney. A trust should be named as a beneficiary to avoid this unnecessary expense and hassle.

Discuss your Plan

Even if you have all your legal documents in place to address disability, incapacity, or death, it is also important that you communicate your wishes to your loved ones and let them know if they have a role in your plan. Let them know where your documents are located, what your special wishes are pertaining to health decisions and decisions regarding your children and loved ones, and where you have documented your assets. Let them know who your advisors are and who to contact in the event something happens.

What's sharing too much? When to talk to your kids.

During this experience, you have seen how important it is to have meaningful conversations with your family about your wishes. Most importantly, this is the time to cherish your loved ones. None of us know when our last day will be. And we also don't know what the future holds for those we love. Today and *now* is when we need to make sure that we treasure every moment and never hesitate to make sure our loved ones know how much they are loved by us.

Roles & Responsibilities

The following is a summary of the common roles in an estate plan and typical responsibilities. I hope this is helpful to you in preparing your estate plan.

Personal Representative

The Personal Representative (PR) is also known as the "executor." The PR's job is to file the Will and appropriate paperwork with the court to be officially appointed as PR. The PR is the only person who has the authority to carry out all of the necessary steps to ensure that your probate assets (individually-owned property, with no designated beneficiary) are properly accounted for, that expenses are paid, and that the balance is distributed to your beneficiaries or your trust pursuant to the terms of your Will. Typically, a PR hires an attorney to assist with the probate process. The PR should be a financially responsible adult, and their appointment lasts about a year.

Power of Attorney (POA)

The agent under the POA has the ability to act on your behalf in all your financial matters and can act on your behalf regarding legal matters. The agent or attorney-in-fact owes you a fiduciary duty which means that the agent must act in good faith for *your* benefit. They should be a financially responsible adult.

Health Care Proxy

The person who is the proxy has the authority to make decisions regarding your health and medical care (to give or to withhold consent) after consulting with your doctors and other health care providers. The proxy may also select a nursing home, hospice, or other residence in accordance with your previously expressed wishes and may sign documents associated with implementing your wishes and health care decisions. It is very important that you discuss your wishes with the proxy so they know exactly what you would want.

Guardian

A guardian is legally responsible for a minor child and has control over the care and day-to-day custody of that child. This role may be temporary (up to 90 days), or permanent (until the child turns 18), and is appointed by the Court. The guardian does not have the power to oversee the child's assets in Massachusetts. Your nominations for these guardian roles are made under your Will.

Trustee

Trustee roles can vary, depending on the situation. The following are common trustee roles in the trusts that I draft for my clients:

Disability Trustee

The role of the Disability Trustee is to manage the trust assets and to provide for the needs of the lifetime beneficiaries, during periods of your disability (which may be temporary or permanent). The Disability Trustee may make distributions from the trust pursuant to the trust language and any letters of instruction you leave.

Administrative Trustee

At your death, the Administrative Trustee's role is to gather, administer, and distribute the trust assets in accordance with the terms of the trust. Some trusts instruct an outright distribution and some instruct that the assets may stay in trust. The Trustee must apply for a new tax identification number, pay your expenses and debts, and file income and estate tax returns. The Administrative Trustee is responsible for managing the trust assets, collaborating with your Personal Representative, and making distributions to your beneficiaries pursuant to the trust. Their job is complete once the trust assets are distributed. This role is temporary and usually lasts about nine months to a year.

If there is an on-going trust for your beneficiaries, the Trustee is responsible for holding the trust property in trust, investing it, filing income tax returns, and making distributions to the beneficiaries (e.g. descendants). As with all trustee roles, it is important to name successor trustees in the event that the initial trustee named is unwilling or unable to serve. The Trustee's role ends either at the time the assets are fully distributed from the trust or at the death of the beneficiary of that trust.

Step Seven Action List
Planning for
Your Loved Ones

☐ Update or prepare your Health Care Proxy and Health Directives.

☐ Update or prepare your Living Will.

☐ Update or prepare your financial Durable Power of Attorney.

☐ Update or prepare your Will.

☐ Discuss with your attorney to determine if a trust would be the best way to transfer your assets to your future heirs.

☐ Update all of your beneficiary accounts.

- Life Insurance
- Retirement accounts
- Pension
- Any financial accounts with a Designated Beneficiary

☐ Discuss your wishes with all of your agents and chosen representatives.

☐ Document what you own and save the list with your estate documents.

Questions to ask when selecting an Estate Planning Attorney

☐ How long have you been in practice?

☐ Do you specialize in estate planning and estate administration?

☐ Please tell me about your interest, background, and experience in the planning field. What percentage of your practice is in estate planning?

☐ How do you define estate planning?

☐ What is your counseling philosophy?

☐ What is your process for working with me to assure that my plan works?

☐ How will you counsel with me to design my plan?

☐ Can you help me coordinate my plan with the other advisors on my team, such as an investment and tax advisor?

☐ How do we assure that my assets are controlled by my instructions contained in my planning documents? Who is responsible for this coordination, you or me?

☐ How do we assure that my plan stays current with changes in the law?

☐ How often do you review plans with clients and communicate status updates?

☐ What is the level of involvement of my family in the planning process?

☐ How do you bill for these services? Are you fee-based or hourly? What are the expenses to maintain and update my legal planning?

- How much will my estate be charged after I am gone?
- What if I am disabled?

☐ What is your record with regard to probate? How long does it take? What does it cost?

- What percentage of your trust-based plans wind up having assets probated? Do you charge differently for these assets?

☐ Do you handle the filing of death tax returns if they are necessary?

- If you do, how do you charge for that service?

☐ What happens if something happens to you the attorney?

☐ How do I prepare for our consultation?

☐ What type of service should I expect from you?

☐ Do you expect any commitments from me?

QUESTIONS YOU MUST ANSWER AND PREPARATION NEEDED FOR YOU TO EFFECTIVELY PURSUE ESTATE PLANNING

☐ What are my planning goals? For example, taking care of my minor children; making sure the process is easy for my loved ones, etc.)

☐ What issues are most important for me to address in my planning?

☐   Who will fulfill the necessary "helper" roles (Trustee, Guardian)?

☐   Do I have a current inventory of assets?

☐   What advisors can I involve in the planning process to more effectively design and implement my plan?

Step-by-Step Journal

Use this journal section to note your feelings, thoughts, and memories.

Here are some ideas that may be helpful starting points:
- ❖ Today when I woke up my first thought was…
- ❖ I had a happy thought today when I remembered…
- ❖ I am looking forward to…

Moving Forward
Toward New Journeys

*"I'm choosing happiness over suffering,
I know I am. I'm making space for the unknown future
to fill up my life with
yet-to-come surprises."*
— Elizabeth Gilbert,
Eat, Pray, Love

When you lose your life partner, your soulmate, and your best friend, it can be unimaginable to think that you will ever find happiness again. For some women, it might make them feel guilty to move on and allow themselves to ever love like that again. And depending on when you are reading this, it still might be too soon. But what I want to ask you to do is one thing—be open to being happy again.

Whether you are guided by faith, spirituality, or your own guiding compass, you must always value your own life. You must care enough about yourself to keep on living and loving and embracing the mysteries of life that await you. Whether you are in your 90s, or in your 20s, as I was, our husbands would never wish for us to spend our remaining days just waiting to die.

If you feel like you are depressed, please seek the help of doctors and therapists who can give you extra support. Do not deny yourself the help you need and deserve. You cannot help others unless you take care of yourself. Just like what is said during the airplane safety announcements—you first have to put on your own oxygen mask before you try to help anyone else. I sincerely hope that the previous chapters helped you overcome some of the fear of the unknown that is created by the arcane workings of our legal and financial systems. The previous chapters were intended to demystify and empower you with knowledge. There may be other steps you need to take because of your unique personal situation. But first, I hope you actually used all the Step-by-Step Journal pages to write down your thoughts during this process, so now you can go back, read, and appreciate how much you have accomplished and grown since you started this book. You are strong, and you have made it through the worst part.

There are many stages in this process, both emotional and practical. I recall wanting to seize each day and live with a new vigor. Before Ron died, he wanted us to learn how to sail and signed us up for a community boating program. I was so afraid of falling into the water and drowning that I got nicknamed "Barnie" because I clung to the boat like a barnacle!

After Ron died, I decided that I wanted to try sailing again. Despite my earlier reluctance, I didn't care whether or not I fell out of the boat now because the worst had already happened. I took a few classes and was amazed by how much I loved it. Learning to sail in Boston Harbor during the summer is a challenge given all the boat traffic, not to mention the airport traffic overhead! Sailing gave me an incredible boost of confidence and a new hobby of learning how to harness the power of the wind. I felt more in control of my circumstances, and was slowing realizing that despite my profound sadness, I was feeling joy again in my life.

Be true to yourself. Listen. Observe. I hope that as you take these steps (and maybe even make them into smaller steps!) you will begin to feel more in control of your situation and begin to realize that this awful experience that befell you has also presented you with an opportunity. An opportunity to reinvent yourself and to try the new things that will bring you closer to the person you were meant to be.